ENDURING
Southern
HOMES

ERIC ROSS

Photographs by EVIN KREHBIEL

GIBBS SMITH
TO ENRICH AND INSPIRE HUMANKIND

RONDA RICE CARMAN DESIGNERS AT HOME

SOUTHERN SPACES

Contents

Acknowledgments

It takes a team of detail-oriented professionals to make my clients' dreams come true. Every day I enlist the help and services of skilled tradespeople to make beautiful rooms appear miraculously, many times in a matter of days, in my clients' homes. These friends and colleagues make me look like a master, and I am truly grateful. My sincere thanks to:

Jackie Roberts at Decorators Workroom for making the most beautiful bedding, draperies and other soft furnishings; thank you for knowing innately how curtains should fall and function so that they stay beautiful for years. Many times you have kept me from delivering some crazy designs I rendered, translating my drawings into pure elegance when they were installed on-site. Here's to creating even more beautiful rooms together for many years to come.

Shirley Hames and the team at Hamshire House International for always working me into your schedule to receive and deliver all the beautiful furnishings that I purchase all over the world. Bringing these treasures into my clients' homes is not an easy feat, and you and your team always give me your best.

Fred Fitzgerald at 7.0 Interior Services for being the best installer there is. From the first time you brought a steamer to a job, I knew you were the only installer I would ever use. Thanks for being so patient with me in getting every window treatment perfect, many times on-site, so that our projects are completed on time and wow our clients.

All the vendors who have partnered with me over the years to provide beautiful products to my clients, and who go over and above the normal business practices and strive for excellence every day. In particular, Wesley Hall Furniture, Thibaut Wallcovering and Fine Furniture, the Robert Allen Duralee Group and Schumacher—you always make me look good.

My editor, Madge Baird, and production designer, Virginia Snow, at Gibbs Smith for helping me create this beautiful collection of photos and stories. Madge, thank you for always telling me your honest opinion and deftly handling my barrage of questions from day one of this project. You succinctly rephrased my ideas into prose that is interesting, readable and informative.

Photographer Evin Krehbiel, for giving me and our team at Eric Ross Interiors your best every time you show up to document one of our projects. Your perspective and undying patience is appreciated more than you will ever know. Photographing so many projects was a labor of love for me, and I know it was for you too because it shows in every beautiful picture.

My former assistant Christine Barker for helping bring so many of the projects included in this book to life and to my current assistant Sydney Collins for seamlessly taking on the responsibility of assisting me. Thanks also for your tireless efforts in bringing this book to fruition. I will forever be grateful for your passion and encouragement to

begin this project and see it through to completion. I cannot thank you enough.

My wife, business partner and best friend, Ruthann Ross. Nothing I do is worth anything until I share it with you. Your unending work, prayers and emotional support for almost twenty-five years have been the greatest blessings in this world. The pages in this book represent all the hopes and dreams we have worked toward together.

I am so glad that I get to share them with you.

Last but never least, I thank all the clients I have had the good fortune to work with over the years. Without you I wouldn't have houses to decorate every day. It is the one thing I do better than any other. Decorating gives my life meaning, and the fact that people pay me to help them create places to enjoy with their friends and families is a blessing I never take for granted.

The Beginning

I have always loved houses. As a boy growing up in a quaint town in Kentucky, I would ride my bicycle for hours, touring various neighborhoods of my small, southern town. Of course, I would always gravitate toward the neighborhoods with the best houses. Most of the areas I perused were those with older homes, and the ones built in the 1920s–1950s were some of my favorites. Like a beautiful overture, they stirred something inside of me. My hometown has quite a variety of styles: English Tudor, Dutch Colonial, and my very favorite—Georgian. There was even one Mediterranean home complete with stucco and a tile roof that would stop me in my tracks. I remember craning my neck to see what the inside was like. These diverse houses of exotic inspiration evoked a trove of aspirational dreams for a boy of twelve. I would wonder, *How are the rooms laid out inside? How large is the foyer? What do the chandeliers look like?*

Twilight was a favorite time to take these tours. It was the time of day when the windows were still open, but the lights would illuminate the insides of the rooms, enabling me to see inside these private homes that were otherwise closed to me. I would spy a woman setting her dining room table and imagine what she was preparing the table for. Was it a small, intimate gathering of friends, or was it going to be a large dinner party? Oh, how I would envision myself creating an atmosphere of elegance and refinement for my would-be guests one day.

Being from a small town where everybody knew everybody, I knew who many of the prominent people were who lived in these homes. For instance, one was the mayor, one a doctor, and one the heir to a century-old beverage bottling company. These homes were magnificent but not what I call "showy," as many homes are today; they had a quiet elegance about them. I would marvel at how they sat perfectly on a knoll as you rode up the street, or how quaint a house looked tucked below the grade of a winding road. One had a magnificent large oak sheltering its sprawling footprint on a green meadow. It was limed, and I remember how bright the white color was, even in the shade. To this day, if I have a client with a shady lot, I always suggest painting the house white so it is revived out of the dark shade. This is something I learned on those long bike rides in summer: there is nothing prettier than white in the shade.

Thus began my love affair with homes. My aunt Napolee many times told the story of how I came into her house one day and announced, "Aunt Nap, you should have blue candles to match the blue trim in your living room." I was ten years old. What ten-year-old boy even cares about candles? I have lacked many things in my life but was never short an opinion. I have been handing out equally pointed and astute decorating advice proudly for the last thirty-five years. The only difference from

childhood is that now people pay me for my opinions!

How does a young boy from a small southern town begin to have such an opinion on interiors? I think it all started with my mother, who was an immaculate housekeeper. My favorite anecdote about our home is that our house was so perfectly decorated that our bathrooms even had matching toilet paper. Who remembers colored toilet paper? Yes, you could actually buy toilet paper that was green, blue, yellow or pink, and my mother was the target demographic. She also liked to have the towels folded just so, the beds made a certain way, the sofa pillows fluffed and styled—you get the idea. She was a true homemaker in the sense that she knew how to run a household, and I was raised within that ideal of the perfect home and had expectations to match. This sense of order makes a home comfortable, but it also makes running a home easier when you have a pattern of how something should be. That formula my mother instilled in me is basically the same one I use today to set up houses for my clients; at this point, it has become second nature.

A perfect home has the furniture masterfully arranged. Our furniture never moved from the first place it was positioned. Once I asked my mother why we didn't ever move our furniture around, to which she quipped, "Because that's where the sofa goes, and that's where the chairs go. Eric, the house was built with the intent of the sofa going on that wall, not any other wall."

That was my first lesson in interior decoration: listen to what the room is telling you. The room will tell you where the sofa should live, where the chairs should live. Too many people fight against the architecture of a room instead of using architecture as a guide. Where is the fireplace? How can the sofa be in a better relation to it? How can I arrange the furniture so it invites entry? How can I accommodate more people in this room? Is there a way to get the visitors closer, to foster conversation? How can we get more lighting? Where will people put their drinks? The answers begin with architecture.

Perhaps it isn't immediately clear where the room is telling you to place the sofa. But like learning any other language, you learn the language of your own home. Learning involves trial and error, research, and paying attention to the flow of your room; this skill is honed over time. I cannot count how many issues of various shelter magazines I have pored over throughout my life. From childhood until now, I have taken the latest issue of any home publication and dissected the rooms printed on the pages to a painstaking degree. Before iPhones enabled me to zoom in on a photo, I was zooming in the old-fashioned way: digging deep into a picture, getting it as close as I could to see the details. I studied interesting arrangements of objects on a cocktail table, or the pleasing composition of two lamps that weren't exactly the same on end tables flanking a sofa. This is an education that has taken a lifetime.

Since my design concepts are based on the premise that a house, through its architecture, will communicate the proper furniture arrangement it should have, I am drawn to the classic arrangement of furniture, art and accessories. Because these concepts are so tried-and-true, they do a lot of the work for me. For example, I love pairs of things—anything. Using pairs is one of the design elements I employ, some might say liberally, to create balance and cohesion. The reason I love pairs is that they just make you feel good. They naturally help create order and symmetry in a room. Using a pair of chairs, a pair of lamps, a pair of urns is simple but effective—they can highlight a focal point or create a focal point where there is none. Especially in a room where there is a lot of visual interest, pairs give your eyes a place to rest.

Many designers and decorators want to design a more dynamic arrangement of art and furniture in their interiors. They set out to create tension in their rooms. But that is not my goal. Mine is for a room to feel good, not shock you into awe. I want my rooms to hone in on a sense of permanence, as if those rooms have existed for a hundred years. I want them to ground you. This lasting quality to my rooms is what I am most proud of. They are rooms that my admirers say stand the test of time. They endure.

Timeless is a word clients often use to describe the homes I create for them. This quality comes from mixing antiques and familiar color schemes with updated fabrics and upholstery. I insist on using antiques in my projects because they give a sense of history to a room you cannot get with new furniture. Antiques tell a story, and even if you don't know the story, it doesn't matter—they tell it anyway. One can imagine where a table came from, or in whose home a rug has lived. When you purchase antiques,

you become a part of that never-ending story. This is both comforting and exciting to me. Antiques also have a time-worn quality. That's something I particularly love about antique rugs. You cannot ruin an antique rug with muddy feet, a spilled glass of wine, or effusions from a sick child or a pet, because they have already been impacted by such things and are the better for the wear. Antique rugs are my favorite antique to use for this reason. They are as durable as workhorses and at the same time works of art. They elevate a room from pretty to sublime.

Of course, it is important that a room be beautiful and comfortable, but it should also feel like home. This is a difficult balance to strike and a quality that can be elusive. When a new client asks me to help them with their home, my goal is to create something they—not I—would be happy living in. I ask myself, *What will this person relate to, get excited about and become inspired by? What do they collect or would they like to collect?* This really gives me insight into their passions and helps create a backstory for their home. By reflecting their tastes and amusements, their new home

will not only feel personal but will surely stand the test of time. Fads do not play a part in my design process; instead I focus on what the client truly loves and wants to share with their family and friends. This makes the rooms persist longer than the "all-white" trend or "modern farmhouse" or any other style of the moment. I may use elements of these trends in a room as inspiration here or there, but I try not to adhere to one design scheme because there is no longevity in it. And quite frankly, interior design is an investment. Clients spend a lot of time and resources on their homes, so they want them to survive the waves of trends and fads.

For me, decorating always starts with the floor plan. I lay out the furniture and begin to imagine walking through the rooms, entertaining in the rooms, welcoming guests to dinner parties and hosting family for the holidays. The stories I tell myself, imagining my clients' families in the spaces, are just an extension of ten-year-old me peddling around small-town Kentucky imagining the families' activities in those homes I so admired. These scenarios help me begin to create the finishes and color scheme. *Does the house need to be casual for a young family or lend itself to a more chic interior for empty-nesters?* Imagining how they will live in it determines the fabrics I select. A durable wool, an outdoor chenille, or a fine silk—these choices are born in how the rooms will be used. Even if the scenarios are my own musings, they are based on knowing my clients, and more generally, how people entertain, celebrate and relax. Knowing how children will come in a back door and run their hands down a hallway determines that they will need a durable yet beautiful wallpaper so handprints aren't overtly visible. Form really does follow function in many of these homes, while some are beautiful expressions of their owners' interests and passions.

I am so pleased to be able to present this collection of homes. Every one is a love story in its own right. The rooms were created from the foundation of all the lessons I learned from hours of bike rides around small Southern neighborhoods and years of searching for and dreaming about every detail from magazines. My clients have allowed me to use a lifetime of imagining to create enduring homes for them and their families. I hope you will be inspired by these rooms and enjoy the stories they tell.

Chapter One

ANTEBELLUM JEWEL

A client and her husband had bought an antebellum property well south of Nashville and had been renovating it for over two years. She was exhausted from the countless decisions they'd had to make over the previous years and just couldn't face making any more. She knew that the decorating would make or break the entire project, so she called to ask if I would help her. I immediately said, "Yes!" After all, it is a jewel in every interior designer's crown to decorate a Southern antebellum mansion. I was eager to help and honored to be asked.

I started with a couple of rooms instead of the whole house. This allowed less commitment from the client emotionally and financially in the beginning and gave us more time to get to know each other. I quickly pulled together a preliminary look, or "mood," for the project and presented it in one room rather than the entire house—which can take months. The client saw that I was achieving her desired look in one or two rooms, which enabled a faster completion of the whole house project in the long run.

The first phase of this project included the living and dining rooms, with the foyer thrown in as a bonus. Even though most foyers are small, they are mighty because they set the tone for the entire look of a home. Here I introduce the colors and themes of the home in microcosm. My inspiration for the foyer in this project came directly from the couple who hired me and from the home's grandeur and sublime setting. The clients were affable and chic, with a penchant for entertaining large groups of friends and colleagues. I wanted to create rooms that were as easygoing and elegant as they were.

The home and its surrounding farm were incredibly romantic. The gate to the property was quite grand, and an allée of trees ended at a round motor court. The architecture of the house was Italianate with farm-style touches, such as a red, standing-seam roof. Barns and rolling hills created a stunning backdrop, yet acted as a counterpoint to the formality of the house itself. This casual elegance was an overarching theme I wanted to communicate through the colors and furnishings.

I decided on a subtle faux finish for the walls in the grand foyer, as I felt a simple coat of paint would feel too new and inauthentic in this environment because of the history and style of the home.

PREVIOUS OVERLEAF: The foyer of the grand home showcases a collection of Imari objects to highlight the clients' rug. The ostrich-leg lamps are reproductions of ones designed by Tiffany. **OPPOSITE:** The pull between traditional fabric and the clean silhouette of the chairs was an embodiment of the homeowners' style: traditional but not stodgy.

I wanted the walls to have a look of age, so I commissioned a talented local artist to produce a smoky effect. My directive was for the walls to look like there had been a fire but all the smoke had been sucked out, leaving only a residue behind. The subtle finish perfectly exudes age and character without being overtly antiqued.

The client had some existing pieces for the foyer: a reproduction antique buffet and a lovely Cajun-shrimp-colored Persian rug. The colors of the rug immediately had me wishing for a massive collection of Imari dishes to pair with it, which is exactly what we found and displayed on the wall above the buffet. I found an amazing large-scale bird-and-flowers print fabric, which looked like a Chinese hand-painted wallpaper, in colors of pale blue, green, coral and navy that also complemented. Though the scale of the print is suited for tall window treatments, the large pattern looked stunning on two clean-lined wing chairs. Thus we had the perfect combination of colors to pull from for the rest of the house.

For the living room, I wanted to contrast the romantic softness I had planned for the dining room, so I amped up the orange from the foyer. A sherbet, gray and white floral fabric for the drapes and pillows did the trick. The upholstery has been covered in a smoky nickel–colored velvet. A tourmaline-glazed cotton on some reproduction French-style chairs added interest to the mix, contributed to the layered look, and prevented a monochromatic effect.

I also commissioned a fun leopard-print knotted rug to kick the chic level up a notch. As an interesting study in textures, I covered the walls in natural sisal but left the paneled millwork. This play between the formal moldings and the rugged sisal augmented the theme of casual elegance for this room.

ABOVE: Etchings of other historic plantations hang over the mantel.
OPPOSITE: Velvet, cotton and sisal mix to create a chic but relaxed atmosphere in the living room. **OVERLEAF:** A daybed is perfectly placed in front of the fireplace for enjoying cozy nights with friends.

The house's north-south exposure is challenging because the shadows make things murky and gray all day. It is difficult to get color, especially paint, to render a true cast in such light. We tried several shades of blue until we landed on the proper hue that enhanced the blue-and-cream embroidered-linen window treatments. An antique Persian Tabriz rug brought just the right balance of formality and age to the room.

To accommodate large parties, I selected a long, oval table in a medium wood tone with antique cream-colored chairs upholstered in a combination of two linens: a quilted turquoise linen and a turquoise-and-taupe leopard print. The animal print contributed a bit of whimsy, and the mixing of finishes signaled less formality. The client's nicely curated collection of oil paintings was the perfect accompaniment to the elegant mood of the room.

Because we limited the scope of our first project, I was able to install these rooms within a short amount of time—approximately eight weeks. The clients were so pleased with the result that they immediately asked me to finish the home.

French antique iron urns were perfectly scaled for the dining table and punctuated the overall feeling of romance in the dining room.

For the husband's study, a grasscloth wall-covering in a warm shade of celadon peppered with brown speckles gave even more subtle texture and was perfectly partnered with a dark brown printed fabric that made the overall feel more masculine. I liked the counterintuitive concept of using celadon, usually thought of as a feminine color, in a man's office. The menswear effect of the pinstripe on the drapes also helped achieve another layer of masculinity.

We reused the client's existing cognac leather club chairs, but I re-covereded the seat cushions in the same printed fabric as the window treatment cornice. I added a freestanding bookcase in black to give more visual weight and sobriety to the light walls. Cobalt blue accents in lamps and objets d'art contributed a lively effect.

OPPOSITE: A hallmark of my work is to create rooms from underutilized spaces. Here, a French table previously used in the clients' kitchen was repurposed in a hallway to create a sitting area. **ABOVE LEFT:** A hallway to the kitchen wing is decorated in blue and white. A shelf with baskets holds dog toys and treats for the homeowners' crew of five rescue dogs. **ABOVE RIGHT:** Small chairs fit nicely in vacant small spots and can be pulled into adjacent rooms as needs arise—a much more elegant option than folding chairs.

The master suite as well as the husband's study were in the same wing and floor, so I wanted all the fabrics and colors to flow effortlessly. I decided on celadon as the main color for both rooms, but to pair celadon with darker grounds for his study, and lighter grounds for the bedroom.

The bedroom was to be soft and romantic, a dreamy retreat. I selected a sumptuous combination of embroidered and printed fabrics along with a plissé velvet and an embroidered border tape trim. The walls of the bedroom were painted in a pure shade of celadon and the bathroom was wallpapered in a metallic silver flora-and-fauna print with tones of charcoal, mint and yellow. I kept the color palette in the bedroom quiet and monochromatic, layering in gray for the upholstered bed and chairs, all sitting atop a celadon tone-on-tone wool area rug. By repeating the gray and celadon colors with cream accents, I kept the overall color scheme neutral and calming.

ABOVE LEFT: The master bed is crowned with a canopy, a must-have in a luxurious bedroom. **ABOVE RIGHT:** One wall of cabinetry was added for additional clothing storage, also allowing for a window bench overlooking the estate. **OPPOSITE:** A small writing desk in the master bedroom is big enough to slip a large dog kennel underneath, for the rescues who like being near their owners. **OVERLEAF:** The classic Brunschwig and Fils pattern was combined with modern accents to make the master bath feel chic and pretty in its traditional setting.

Helping to decorate a 150-year-old antebellum mansion was a joy and a real exercise in collaboration. The client painstakingly chose all the architectural layouts and finishes while leaving me the opportunity to inject visual panache with elegant curtains, furnishings and wall treatments. This is a home where the clients can breathe easy and entertain for many years to come.

Worth Noting

* Selecting paint colors can be tricky because the direction the light enters a room makes a difference in how colors display in your home. In a room with low or no natural light (say, a north-facing room), shadows will make colors look cooler than they looked at the paint store. The opposite is true of a west-facing room that gets a long exposure to sun; the sun will add its own heat to whatever color is painted on the walls. A south-facing room probably gives the truest representation of color.

* Always test paint colors in the rooms that will actually be painted to assure you are getting the color you want. Running the test paint into a corner will give you a truer picture of how the color will look, since the shadows will intensify once all the walls are covered. If you have cooler shadows, you'll want to select a paint color that has warm overtones.

* When decorating a historic home, be the consummate host by choosing comfortable and beautiful furnishings rather than going for a full period look. A room with too many period furnishings can set an austere mood that is off-putting to many people. One easy remedy is to pair a nontraditional rug with formal furnishings, which makes the room feel more approachable to guests.

Chapter Two

A FRENCH EMBRACE

When a client asked for my help in downsizing from her large home—which I had previously decorated with the heavy drapes, swags, fabrics and furnishings that were an ode to Country French—I thought it would be a good opportunity to update her look. The new home was a quaint little duplex located in a retirement community, approximately half the size of her former residence. It was lacking architectural detail and ornamentation and felt more like a condo than a grand, custom-built home. Since she was a long-time client whose homes had always turned out quite splendidly, I wanted this new home to have a grand feel even though it was rather compact.

It was a challenge to know where to begin, as each room I saw seemed more basic and underwhelming than the one before. When I say "basic," I mean beiges and almonds with oak cabinetry. So together we decided to introduce some cosmetic customization. It needed more than a coat of paint and new carpet and cabinets to achieve a feeling of grandeur. My first decision was to enlarge all the doorways to eight feet tall; this change alone gave the rooms and the whole house the overall effect of seeming larger and more stately.

Because all the client's immediate family lived nearby, she didn't need to use the duplex's three bedrooms as guest rooms. So I decided to outfit the front bedroom—directly off the foyer and living room—as a library for part of her large collection of books. While increasing door heights in this room, I also increased the width of the opening with a pair of eighteen-inch French doors.

The client wanted her new home to be modern and polished. The story I decided on was to make it feel like a Parisian apartment in an old neoclassical walk-up. So I selected beautiful blond-finish French oak hardwood floors, which became a springboard for an overall color scheme for the home.

I started with the temporary (easily changeable) finishes of fabrics, rugs and furnishings. My overall color palette was soft, silvery celadon on the walls, with fabrics of teal, aqua and citrine. This was essentially a modern take on the classic French color scheme of blue and yellow.

The neutral palette emulated the soft focus of a Monet painting. I describe this effect as *milky*: I want the rooms to appear as if we brushed a milky film across them. In new homes, this romantic color palette helps give the rooms a sense of patinaed venerability.

ABOVE AND OPPOSITE: Mixing traditional accessories with modern fabrics generates a dynamic effect in the living room. **OVERLEAF:** The dining room is open to the living room, so I repeated the fabrics from the pillows on the chairs. A small antique Swedish bench provides more seating. The client and I found the vintage chinoiserie wall panels on a shopping trip together.

Another major change to the duplex came by opening up the kitchen to the great room and breakfast room, which not only improved visual access but the overall traffic flow, so the kitchen and breakfast room work for serving and entertaining guests.

We indulged in custom cabinetry for the kitchen. I specified roasted marshmallow as the color, to pick up on the soft tan highlights of the floor.

OPPOSITE: A small breakfast table looks into the living room. I re-covered the client's existing armchairs to match the new color scheme and added a new breakfast table to match the kitchen cabinets. Using similar finishes in a room makes the room feel larger.

Carrying on the theme of grandeur, we decided to splurge in the powder room with a hand-painted wallpaper of flora and winged fauna from Gracie. This creates a surprise moment of opulence for the visitor. The large scale of the paper transforms this ordinary, two-piece powder room into an enchanted garden; the entire room is a focal point. Since the client is an avid admirer of birds, this paper is the perfect appurtenance to the home and adds a personal touch.

Lighting was another major factor in designing this space. Well-chosen lighting is like jewelry for the home. It is the one area in decorating that I think is always worth the splurge. It matters not only that the light is beautiful but also that it is of good quality and in proper scale. For example, a chandelier that is too small looks cheap, and one that is too large looks cartoonish and garish. I chose a lot of armed chandeliers with curves and scrolls and lovely dripping decoration. Some were crystal, some silver and gold and wood, but all paid tribute to the French theme.

OPPOSITE: The master bedroom houses a favorite antique portrait flanked by antique French lamps. The master bed is dressed in modern fabrics for a new phase of life.

Downsizing can create a lot of emotions in a client. It can be exciting; it can be overwhelming; it can be challenging. It is difficult enough to sort through all the years of collecting and storing to decide what you keep and what to donate. Most people will just settle for a smaller and unnoteworthy space in which to retire. But this client wanted something with the panache and style she enjoys, so we took a basic duplex and injected a *joie de vivre*. By selecting custom finishes and choosing natural materials and soft colors, we were able to take this simple duplex and make it splendid! It works so perfectly for her now. It is convenient and low-maintenance, but it has all the elegance and sophistication of a Paris apartment.

OPPOSITE: A cast-limestone mantel we added to the living room complements the gold-leaf-and-mercury-glass chandelier. All together, the materials used in the home are perfect for a chic French setting.

Worth Noting

Choice of materials and appointments elevated this nondescript home to a chic residence for someone who likes to entertain. Here are the takeaways:

* Choose materials that enhance the story you want your home to tell. Perfectly chosen chandeliers, floors and fabrics make a big difference.

* Splurge on finishes that you will live with for a while, like beautiful French oak floors and upgraded lighting.

* Create an all-over color palette for smaller homes and stick with it throughout the entire space to create a unified look. This fools the eye into thinking the home is larger than its actual square footage.

Chapter Three

COLONIAL ENCORE

New homes are much more accommodating for modern living than old-home renovations are: you can design them with large closets, bathrooms and pantries—even bright basements. But they can be devoid of the character and the proper grandeur of a Southern mansion.

This client couple adores old homes and are enamored with the historic character of their hometown of Franklin, Tennessee, where arguably one of the bloodiest battles of the Civil War was fought. It has a charming town square. Old homes line the shady streets and create a storybook setting, and it was among these homes that my clients developed their new-home architecture. This was my directive from the couple: Give us a gracious, traditional Southern mansion with large, comfortable rooms to entertain loads of family and friends. I knew what to do: The true hallmark of a Southern home is comfort.

The charming wallcovering in the foyer, with its toss of shamrocks and red flowers, adds a historic look to the newly built home.

Southern hospitality requires that the guest be offered a drink upon entering the home, so having a bar, especially in the living room, is very important. There needs to be a place where you can set up a small tray with whiskey, gin, and vodka with sodas. If you have room for mixers too, great! But at least set up a small tray for liquor and a bowl of nuts. This simply communicates, "We are glad you are here and have set up some refreshment for you." A small bar set-up instantly turns down the fussy and turns up the effortlessness. For that reason, in the formal living room of this house we placed a game table with a pair of chairs and a small drinks cabinet nearby. This gracious sign of welcome is the first thing one sees from the foyer.

A key piece of furniture that makes a room feel relaxed, and therefore more Southern, is a footstool or an ottoman—or both and in multiples. This is another cue for your guest to make herself comfortable. An otto-man can be used as a quick seat for an impromptu conversation or as a place to put up your feet and rest. In more formal rooms, this is especially important. It is also a great place to use an animal print, and if you use one in a playful color instead of a literal animal skin, it can turn up the charm as well. I used a blond cheetah epingle fabric on a chair and a pair of footstools in this room for a bit of whimsy. One of my favorite stories about animal prints is when a client asked me, "Eric, aren't you afraid that animal print will go out of style?" To which I quipped, "It's been in style since the time of Napoleon; I think you are good."

The study is almost always an opportunity to create a visual counterpoint to the formality that I generally imbue in foyers and living spaces. I like the effect of using the same color on walls and trim, especially a dark color.

For this client, I went with a moody, bluegrass green on all the trim and walls. It generates a feeling of richness—almost of velvet—and imparts a sense of heaviness—a masculine touch. I used the dark matching color on all the bookcases as well.

In an unusual exception, I opted for two-inch mahogany wood blinds instead of fabric window treatments in order to give the room a vintage feel. I also placed a mahogany desk and chair in front of one wall of bookshelves. The red tone of the wood against the juniper-like green casework produces a rich, dynamic look.

Just one, William Morris–inspired, printed fabric was used in the room, coupled with leather, to finish off the look. Instead of a traditional antique Persian rug, which I always love, I chose a blond antelope. It injects a fresh, younger look so the room feels like a historic interpretation rather than a literal reproduction.

PREVIOUS OVERLEAF: A small sofa flanked by two bookcases in the living room creates an intimate seating area in the large room. **OPPOSITE:** A handsome sitting area next to the bookshelves across from the desk is a good place for conversation or quiet reading.

In the heart of the home is the den, which I designed on the theme of a cigar lounge that gentlemen would have moved to after dinner. Along with shades of cognac and whiskey with touches of black and red, the combination of colors and furnishings promotes a masculine scene. Plaid velvet on the chairs and wool flame stitch pillows set against walls the color of dark truffle make the clients feel wrapped in a cashmere blanket.

A reproduction hunt board and the clients' own collection of horse paintings turned up the volume on equestrian style, and it couldn't be more perfect. With the house set amid a horse riding school and stables, the nod to American horse style keeps the look authentic.

LEFT: A reproduction hunt board grabs attention between two plaid wing chairs. **ABOVE:** Embroidered ikat pillows add a punch of color to the somber tones of the den.

ABOVE: A wool-covered bench in front of the den fireplace offers additional seating when the homeowners entertain. BELOW: Hand-colored lithographs of deer and elk brighten a dark corner. OPPOSITE: A secretary from the clients' personal collection partners perfectly with equine portraiture. The barrel-back chair has been re-covereded in the ikat fabric used on the pillows in this room.

Entrance to the formal dining room is through double pocket doors, which were chosen as a nod to the double parlor of many Southern homes and as a way to keep the dining room out of view until it's time to reveal the table when dinner is ready. The dining room was one of the first rooms I decorated for the project, and it set the tone for the entire house.

When I was sourcing to decorate the home, I was lucky to find a beautiful set of dining chairs upholstered in a raspberry Pierre Frey velvet check. I don't think you could get more beautiful words in one sentence: raspberry-Pierre-Frey-velvet-check—dreamy, right? I have to admit I was seduced and decided to use raspberry as a subtle accent in all the other rooms, with the crescendo being the chairs around the dining table, as this is one of the last rooms you see in the first floor. Ten raspberry-red velvet check chairs around a dining table is a statement, and they are glorious in their habitat. Legend also has it that red makes you hungry, which is, of course, perfect in the dining room.

On the entire back portion of the house are the breakfast room and kitchen. For this couple's lifestyle, they wanted the working portion of the kitchen separate from the entertaining spaces. The breakfast area is surrounded with windows, letting in dazzling sunlight. Vivid greens of the grass and the trees become part of the kitchen scene. I selected a pale duck-egg blue for the kitchen walls and a buffalo check featuring this color for the chairs. This same color coats the ceilings in the main floor of the house, as a nod to the tradition of painting Southern porches blue.

Below the cabinets, a basket weave tile pattern on all the backsplash made a cleaner look than would interrupting it with decorative liners and inset panels. This is my only non-Southern nod, because we all know that restraint is not a Southern attribute. A leathered black pearl granite on the perimeter cabinets gives the velvety appearance of soapstone without the cost and maintenance, while a contrasting veined granite was a focal point on the island. I like the contrast of dark countertops with light cabinets, as it gives a nice line that draws your eye along the length of the cabinetry, highlighting the millwork.

An arabesque lattice pattern fabric highlights the pretty silhouette of the quintessentially traditional wingback chairs. Budding quince in the vase announces the beginning of spring.

Walking among the rooms of this reinterpreted colonial manse gives one the feeling of grandeur and comfort in a truly Southern style. The size and scale of the rooms are grand, but the furnishings and finishes were chosen for a sense of ease, so that visitors want to stay a while. As you move among the gracious rooms, they evoke a familiar sense of serenity through thoughtful color and pattern choices with style that is rooted in Southern tradition. Yes, this house is a grand Southern mansion, but it is a home set up for modern entertaining for all who have the pleasure of being invited in as friends.

Worth Noting

These are my favorite tips for creating a Southern Colonial home filled with an expression of warmth:

✳ Nothing says welcome like a tray of drinks or a drink station. Just by setting up a tray of liquor, mixers and a salty snack you give your guests the sense that you are happy to welcome them in your home.

✳ Use rich, warm colors instead of cool, gray tones. Southerners are not known for their subtlety, so color schemes should be bold and enveloping at the same time. Red with brown is a tried-and-true color combination that looks wonderful with rich woods such as mahogany and walnut.

✳ Don't forget to paint your ceilings. In this home, timeless duck-egg blue imbues a sense of Southern style as a nod to historic porch ceilings. Blue ceilings are unexpected and lend a nostalgic touch. Be careful to pick a quiet shade that is easy to live with.

Chapter Four

AN ODE TO CHIPPENDALE

When I met with the clients of this new home, a husband and wife who had previously owned an antiques booth, I was delighted that they wanted me to completely decorate their new home as I saw fit. And, by the way, could I please use all the wonderful antiques they had collected over the years? I was thrilled.

The entire house was a treasure trove of collections piled high. All the rooms had amazing pieces of furniture, art and objets d'art they had curated though the years. I was bursting with ideas of what we could do. As I rounded the corner from their living room into their large, centrally located kitchen, I stopped dead in my tracks. Their kitchen opens onto a charming breakfast room to one side and a keeping room to the other. There were windows everywhere and the light streamed in from all directions.

My eyes quickly focused on a set of dining chairs with needlepoint seats that I had seen at a favorite antique store just days before. Finding them now at home at this project was kismet. I couldn't wait to begin decorating.

The foyer and dining room in this house are, for all intents and purposes, the same room. In the dining room, they had just acquired a new Chippendale table and had also bought new dining chairs in this style. They had a pair of austere portraits of a man and woman dressed in black that the client wanted to place in the foyer. The husband had also acquired a very beautiful and delicate antique crystal chandelier with bobeches and crystal drops to be hung over the dining table. But to my eye, all of this fussiness could be off-putting to visitors. So I thought we needed to set all of these fancy finds in a more livable, approachable backdrop. The challenge was to celebrate these beautiful finds while dressing them down for more contemporary living.

One design device I employ is to mix rough and fine, high and low. It is in the intersection of this juxtaposition where a room becomes livable, approachable and comfortable. Fine wool and silk can be mixed with the rough facade of pine or cypress, or glossy chintz can be mixed with drab, dark walls. This brings a twenty-first-century sensibility to traditional style, art and antiques.

For this couple's overly elaborate dining room, I chose a backdrop of sisal wallcovering. Predictably, I received pushback from the clients and had to do quite a tap dance to convince them not to choose silk damask for the walls. I acquiesced to covering a small niche in the foyer, and one in the dining room where the sideboard would reside, in a soft metallic wallpaper of flora and fauna if they would allow me to install sisal. This would give them the elegant touch they wanted while conveying a more relaxed mood in the dining room. The result was a beautiful foyer and dining room that provided a warm welcome to visitors.

Mother and father portraits soberly welcome guests to this home, while metallic floral wallpaper brightens up the otherwise somber mood.

The living room was another area where hyper-formality could have taken center stage. I quickly discerned that my clients envisioned a home that was ripped out of the pages of *Pride and Prejudice*. This is very common among antiques lovers: The romance of beautiful antiquities can lead to period decorating, because the objets d'art seemingly demand it. But as their collection grows, they become less concerned with comfort and focus than with staying true to the era from which they are collecting. This rigid adherence to a period or style makes rooms feel stuffy and formal, as if you are in a museum instead of a home.

The clients' own sofa was a camelback with Chippendale-style legs, and they also had a Martha Washington chair. Since these pieces are both very stiff-looking, I slipcovered the sofa in a soft blue linen with a worn floral print to moderate all the harsh, straight lines. In my opinion, most period rooms are very "leggy," so adding a skirt subdues the formality and adds charm and approachability to the overall look. Normally I don't take the slipcover skirt to the floor, but rather add a six-to-ten-inch skirt, which shows off the pretty, carved legs while adding the needed softness.

To the living room I also added a new Oriental-style rug with a more open field, which gave a lighter feel. The fabric chosen for the window treatments was a modern leaf embroidery in cream and terra-cotta with touches of robin's-egg blue that complemented the blue ceiling and provided a soft backdrop for the mahogany finishes of the case goods.

LEFT: Figuring out the furniture puzzle was compounded by the fact that Mr. Client had an affinity for the Chippendale style and possessed a lot of sofas and chairs in this design. The repetition of the same style made it a challenge to create diversity, so this is where fabrics really came into play.

The formal living room looks onto a covered porch that takes the soft terra-cottas and blues of the living room and turns up the volume. In my experience, outdoor spaces that are in proximity to formal rooms can be the hardest to decorate. Choosing colors for the outdoors that are too loud can distract from the visual impact of the adjacent room; on the other hand, a sea of cream can be underwhelming and unimaginative.

Here I used the same colors as in the living room but just made them juicier—oranges and teals but with traditional accents of blue-and-white Chinese export porcelain. We also used some of the clients' solid wood antiques that were really not rated for the outdoors, but since the porch was enclosed on three sides, we determined they would be fine. Those interior pieces helped lend an interior feel to the outdoor room.

OPPOSITE: A bright stripe gives life to the entertaining space on a porch that was particularly dark. Blue and white with touches of orange are a classic porch color scheme, allowing Chinese export porcelain to reign supreme.

The real heart of this home is the large, open space encompassed by the kitchen, breakfast room and keeping room. I decided to layer in some playful prints in chocolate, blue and rust, which complemented the lighter blue, terra-cotta and cream in the more formal front rooms. Playing with and creating different variations of colors and prints really allowed us to showcase the clients' collection of Mulberry, Imari and, of course, Chippendale-style furnishings.

We reupholstered the existing camelback sofa (next page) in a black-brown and gray glen plaid. The wing chair is covered in the same glen plaid, accompanied by a fabric with a yellow toss of flowers in a charming colonial style; I also added a nailhead trim to give it a masculine note. All the mixing and matching created a casual mood in which the family could relax with each other.

OPPOSITE: These antique chairs had caught my eye at a local antique store. Little did I know that the client had purchased them for this home even before we met! **ABOVE LEFT:** An enfilade shows how mocha, terra-cotta and blue were worked together to create a classic tableaux among the keeping room, breakfast room and kitchen. **ABOVE RIGHT:** The clients' collections are perfectly at home in the breakfast room, where the crisp white backdrop allows the treasures to shine.

LEFT: Needlepoint is a perfectly traditional touch against the shrimp-colored leopard-print bergère chair. The French style of the chair brings a Continental flair to the otherwise English keeping room. RIGHT: Layering of patterns, colors and textures is used to full effect here. A subtle damask-style wallcovering gives more texture to the room than mere paint would.

The master bedroom was a great part of the project because we were able to depart from the formality of the first floor. The clients had visited a showhouse room I had done and fell in love with the lead fabric and overall color scheme of blue and citrine, so I replicated the look for them in their master suite.

The lead print for the bedroom and bathroom was a navy, peacock-blue and citrine Oriental print. I found a Chinese Chippendale bamboo lattice-pattern wallpaper for the bathroom and repeated it on the bedroom ceiling as a linking element. The overall effect was a masculine and traditional space that both husband and wife loved.

OPPOSITE: A reproduction Audubon shorebird print is the centerpiece to this modern take on Southern tradition.
RIGHT: Remnants of the pillow fabric from the sitting area sofa have been turned into artwork above the master bed.

I'll never forget the night I delivered the sofa for the formal living room. My upholsterer, with whom I have worked with for the entirety of my decorating career, was backed up with dozens of pieces, and it was the holiday season, so he just could not get the slipcover completed in time for my install. I went ahead and installed the room without the sofa. The clients were okay with waiting, but they were having their Christmas party the next week, and I wanted them to have the room completed for their guests. I begged my upholsterer to please have the sofa ready for this party. He met the deadline, but I literally delivered the sofa through the rear door as the guests were arriving in the front of the house. It was a seamless hand-off between my clients and me, as I discreetly ducked out the back with my upholsterer.

The house functioned just as we had planned, showcasing their lifetime of collections in a livable way for them and their friends to enjoy.

Worth Noting

* Thomas Chippendale was from England, and his style was often replicated in Colonial times. There are many American antiques that were made as copies of this beloved English design, which is why it is frequently found in antiques stores, from Sotheby's to local flea markets. If you look around your own home, you will probably find that you have one or more of these pieces.

* The graphic nature of Chinese Chippendale has a modern quality that can make rooms less stuffy. The angularity of the pattern is a nice relief to floral patterns and brings freshness to otherwise formal spaces. It is a timeless element you can add to any traditional room to give it levity.

Chapter Five

EQUESTRIAN ESCAPE

Some projects are once-in-a-lifetime opportunities that come at the right place and time. I have always loved the romantic idyll of farm living but had never designed an entire farm. So, when a new client reached out to me to help design a new construction farmhouse in a golf course neighborhood, I was intrigued and signed on.

The unique aspect of this project was that the client and her husband had recently purchased a double lot on which to locate a mini farmstead. She also wanted to include a few outbuildings and a vegetable garden, along with cutting gardens so that it would be in the manner and romance of a small working farm. The rear of the home would face the golf course, while the front would face a large grazing pasture leased by an equestrian school.

The client had already worked with an architect to lay out the rooms in a traditional manner and to create a formal Colonial elevation. She liked the large rooms but wanted them to feel more intimate; she wanted a brighter kitchen and improved movement among the public rooms. The kitchen was to be in the center of the house, between the great room and the dining room. This orientation would make the kitchen dark, because the windows were located on the opposite end of the dining room. I suggested swapping the dining room and kitchen locations to gain all the light from the rear of the house for the kitchen. We could also bump out the kitchen a bit to make it larger, adding Dutch doors on either side, one to the covered porch and one to a side porch that led out to what would be a raised vegetable garden.

I started my decor scheming with the kitchen area. As we redesigned a much larger kitchen with vaulted ceilings and overlooking the golf course, we decided on a bank of windows over the sink and a clerestory window above, allowing for as much natural light as possible.

To counteract all the volume created by the vaulted ceilings, I chose a multitude of finishes for this farm-style kitchen. Brick, stone, wood and ceramic tile were employed in large amounts to create as much interest as possible. All the different surfaces generated patterns and textures to bring the space into human-scaled proportions.

A stone-clad inglenook was designed to house a buttercream, enameled AGA range. This created a romantic story that the space was once the cooking fireplace, where iron kettles hung from forged-iron swing arm hooks. We applied a brick facade on either side of the range nook, which makes it appear as if this wall was the exposed brick from the outside wall, creating a more casual and humble feel to the kitchen and dining room areas. My client was at first hesitant to use so many materials, but she was won over when she saw all the finishes installed together with the wallcovering and other fabrics.

For this project, I had originally envisioned a farmstead overlooking the Hudson River in New York. For my first round of selections, I chose soft blues, quiet celadon greens and terra-cottas for the fabrics and wallcoverings. After presenting them to the client, she said, "Eric, these are all very pretty and I know it would be lovely when you finished the home, but I really want something brighter and more casual." I quipped, "This farmhouse isn't in Kansas." To which she replied, "My grandmother was from Kansas." Unfazed, I quickly said, "Well, let's do a Kansas farmhouse then." And we completely upped the color volume and turned down the formality.

In the dining room, a coral floral print fabric was used to re-cover the client's existing dining chairs, as a bright counterpoint to the dark russet-colored exposed brick wall on the far end of the dining room. I found an extensive collection of antique green and white transferware to display in the built-in shelves that lined the two walls of the dining room.

ABOVE: The colors in the antique Sultanabad rug lead the eye into the dining room, where exposed brick contributes a masculine feel and floral chairs provide a feminine aura.

For the great room, I dressed the hearth area in field-stone and incorporated a beadboard detail for the mantel and overmantel. To give more character to the massive room, I designed a geometric pattern in oversized wood trim for the ceiling. This injected an elevated style to the room while also communicating vintage charm. The walls were painted a shade of burlap, and we used a combination of cotton stripes, wool plaids and mohair atop an immense antique Persian Sultanabad to create a feeling of warmth. The combination of all the patterns, colors and textures makes this room one of the favorites I've ever done!

ABOVE: I stumbled across the most amazing bronze mirror with primitive tulips around the frame, all overpainted in verdigris, for above the game table. **RIGHT:** I chose an ikat fabric for the single club chair in the living room. It adds a zing to the room like a pocket square does to a man's blazer.

The foyer extends in front of the great room and is alive with the most colorful, Jacobean-style wallcovering. This room cheerfully greets every guest with its bright and bold color scheme. I selected a large dentil molding cornice detail to create a formal English theme for the architecture. For furnishings, I used the client's previous round game table as a center hall table and found an old and distressed Welsh cupboard to house an antique china collection.

OPPOSITE: A small green-painted antique chair complements the coral and green colors in the wall-covering. **ABOVE:** During a preconstruction meeting, I advocated making the mudroom two stories so we could have a dormer above to let in more light. Up high is the perfect place to set the antique rocking horse. Brick gives a sense of history and never shows dirt.

The master bedroom suite has a bucolic golf course view. For a relaxed and cozy mood, I chose a combination of cream and aqua print fabrics, mostly linen. A large paisley print employed as a band detail enlivened the striped window treatments. I selected a smaller scale flora and fauna wallpaper in cashew and cream for the accent wall behind the bed as well as in the bathroom to link the two spaces.

LEFT: An antique painting of an Australian sheep farm is a tongue-in-cheek sleep inducer in this master bedroom. **ABOVE:** The flora and fauna silhouette wallcovering has a Southern vibe and softens the master bath, which combines traditional and modern finishes.

For the guest rooms, we developed two different looks. A primitive-style quilt the client had was the springboard for one of the rooms. Its colors were petal pinks, creams and blues, I found the perfect bird-and-floral fabric to lead with, complemented with a simple window-pane plaid and a mini-floral for the bed.

OPPOSITE: The client's existing antique quilt inspired the color scheme of the main-floor guest suite. LEFT: I love how this free-standing cabinet in the bathroom makes the room feel more luxurious and less utilitarian. BELOW: The guest suite opens to the front porch, allowing bucolic views of the horse farm.

In another guest room, sunflower yellow was the primary color. For a farm, sunny yellow is a must, and I thought a guest room would be the perfect place for it. I painted the en-suite bathroom cabinetry all in sunflower yellow, and to tie in, I chose a yellow grout for the white tile—adding a custom touch that you don't notice immediately. For the fabrics, I selected a modern flame stitch print in shades of gray, white and yellow. Layering makes this room appear as if it was thrown together from different times rather than created all at once.

LEFT: The lavender toss pillow on the bed breaks up the yellow and gray palette. **ABOVE:** One of my favorite bathrooms: the yellow cabinets and penny round tile tells a vintage tale.

Of all the houses I have ever designed and decorated, the look and feel of this home is one of my favorites. Its combination of colors, textures and fine materials created a stately but still comfortable home. With an amassed collection of old and new furnishings and immaculate attention to the details of various building materials, the result was an awe-inspiring farmhouse that is at once elegant and relaxed in its finishes and proportions.

Worth Noting

* Making a large room feel intimate is especially challenging. I find the easiest trick is to paint them a dark color. Dark colors advance, making the walls feel like they are closer to you. This method is effective in two-story rooms with a lot of light.

* Using multiple finish materials takes a deft hand. You need to consider the proportions of a room to figure out if all the various materials you may want to use will work. Using various materials en masse and in fairly equal balance will keep the room from looking busy. This way, materials support each other and one doesn't dominate.

* Look for ways to personalize a space, evoking memories. This nod to a home-owner's personal history is what gives character to an interior that decorating with random objects cannot.

Chapter Six

A BELGIAN MANSE

Several themes have emerged in my design work over the years: heavy layering of fabrics and textures, contrasting color schemes, and pretty rooms in traditional color palettes, to name a few. So when a client called to request that I help them create and decorate a Belgian farmhouse, I was intrigued at the new opportunity. The Belgian farmhouse style has been a super-hot look for almost ten years now. While not a new fad in Europe, it is definitely one in the States. The style is all about neutral colors and heavy textures. It's about mixing stone and wood with linen and pale colors, usually some anemic shade of gray, beige, or greige. I saw the prospect of designing and decorating an entire 8,000-square-foot home this way as a challenge. How could I work within very tight color and style boundaries but still make a home visually interesting on such a large scale? I was eager to begin.

The husband and wife clients began their project without an interior designer, thinking they could make all the selections themselves. This is a common thought among people building custom homes. They begin the process with a home builder and are quickly overwhelmed by all the choices they have to make. What kind of roofing material do you want? What color will the roofing material be? How long do you want the roofing material to last? What kind of flashing do you want to use, copper or metal? And these are just the questions that arise for the roof! The difficulty of making all of these choices had put the clients behind schedule, and they asked me to bring their vision to life.

I began by asking lifestyle questions of the couple and their blended families. They wanted the home to be a haven for their children and friends. They asked for multiple entertaining areas, a bar for serving drinks and a kitchen opened to the living area. As I reviewed the floor plan they had developed with the architect, I noticed that the large first floor had very limited cased openings, meaning all the rooms were essentially one large room, with wings that went in different directions. There was just one large room with a kitchen at one end, living space at the other end and dining area in the center. The home was all open, more like a large open-plan loft than a house.

95

I suggested that having an entrance to each room would give the house a sense of stature, a more noble mood fitting its size and design. If we created cased openings between the different areas, this would give each space a sense of being its own room, rather than having an open, loft feel.

Between the kitchen and living room, I designed a pair of cased openings flanking a large peninsula of cabinetry in the center, which can be used as a station for serving food during parties. The two points of entry allowed for great flow and maintained open sight lines. I also added a cased opening between the living and dining rooms. I divided the bar area with cased openings and a custom cabinetry serving station so that a bartender could serve from behind it. I recommended this design because this family could use it as a bar but also style it as a butler's pantry when they resell the residence later. What started as one large room with four different zones was now four separate rooms: living room, kitchen, dining room and bar. Creating deliberate rooms also allowed me to design various ceiling treatments where I could use pecky cypress, which has a lot of visual interest and texture due to its pitted surface and light color.

To create intimate spaces out of such the large expanse of rooms that comprised the hub of the home, I normally would use dark colors in contrasting schemes. But because we were limited to keeping the rooms all neutral, I had to deploy more covert decorative schemes. I selected sheer embroidered fabric in a flowing vine pattern for the living room window treatments to soften the hardness of the exposed pecky cypress on the ceiling and the stone fireplace inglenook. The pattern gave a busy visual effect, contributing more texture without feeling heavy.

For the upholstery, a mix of velvet, linen and embroidery with wood beading supplied texture and pattern play, creating interest and making the room feel cozy. I placed two 9 x 13-foot Oushak-style rugs side by side to make one large 13 x 18-foot area rug. The large footprint added softness and a dark contrast to all the ethereal colors of the rooms.

The living room is a study in texture. I designed the inglenook to create more visual interest in the architecture.

For the kitchen, I designed a stone accent wall against the cream strié cabinetry for textural interest. In the dining room, I clad the exterior wall in panels of pecky cypress to contrast the otherwise light walls and window treatments. The complete effect of wood, stone, linen and velvet created the perfect amount of allure among the rooms so that they feel effortless and stylish whether hosting the family for lounging or friends for formal cocktail parties.

OPPOSITE: Stone, wood and metal create visual delight in this kitchen. **BELOW:** Pecky cypress walls in the nook I created at the end of the dining room give the room more depth. Demilune consoles open to full round tables that can be used for additional seating.

The house has a unique floor plan, adding intrigue for me. The foyer is a turreted room at one and a half stories. I set about creating intimate details for the foyer, adding large-scale brackets in pecky cypress, which brought the oversized sense of scale down to a more personal size and helped make the space feel more intimate. A floor of reclaimed French brick interlocked with European white oak created texture.

OPPOSITE: Since the color scheme for Belgian farmhouses is mostly gray, beige and in between, the home needed a lot of texture to vary the overall look and provide layered appeal.

The study, to the left of the foyer, needed to be dressed up enough for a public space, but also for personal space, since it is off the master suite. As a counterpoint I wrapped the room in a blue-black faux barnwood wall-covering. I used a favorite Japanese-inspired cloud-print fabric in the same color scheme to create a cocoon effect. A small beverage center out of sight off the foyer could be used as a coffee station or wine bar, or both! There is seating for two to enjoy the television discreetly placed in the bookshelves, also painted blue-black. The effect is moody, masculine and chic—perfect for the first room you see off the foyer.

ABOVE LEFT: The beverage area in the study. ABOVE RIGHT: Two leather club chairs just beyond the master bedroom are for the couple to enjoy TV. OPPOSITE: The barn-wood walls are covered in vinyl that looks like old wood.

The master suite was a study in restrained French decoration. Belgian linen was a good choice for upholstering the bed and bergère chairs. A quiet, humble ticking stripe seemed right for the window treatments, while blanketing a wool sisal rug with a leopard-print area rug added a zesty spirit to the room. The different layers of pattern and texture made the room delicate but not fussy. A chinoiserie-inspired print for pillows on the bed gave the room a pop of color.

For the master bath, I designed his and her vanity areas in a combination of chrome sink stands, wooden cabinetry, and glass hutches. Shirred café curtains inside the glass cabinets hid unsightly bathroom storage and gave another layer of texture.

The combined effect of all the materials used in the master bath is a quiet, restrained elegance. When working in a neutral palette, changing textures and materials creates eye appeal.

I had never painted an entire house the same color until this one—and it was an undistinguished shade of beige! One of my favorite anecdotes from this project comes from a phone call I received from the husband. He asked, "When are they going to stop painting the walls with primer and paint an actual color on the wall?" I responded, "That *is* the color of the walls." He was speechless. Of course, his wife already knew this. I think he was building a French chateau, but she and I were building a Belgian farmhouse.

With quiet colors and interesting textures and finishes, we designed a home that is impressive in its stature but intimate in its function and feel, making both husband and wife happy in the end.

OPPOSITE: The covered terrace directly off the formal living room allows for al fresco entertaining when the weather permits. RIGHT: The bamboo-style host chair is actually faux-painted aluminum, which will resist the elements.

Worth Noting

✳ When working within a certain design theme, look for elements from other themes to add a unique take on the aesthetic. For the master bedroom in this project, I added a chinoiserie floral—not commonly seen in a Belgian farmhouse—to inject color and pattern, giving the room a unique element.

✳ If you have an open floor plan, consider how can you make your singular area have multiple personalities to give the overall look more interest. Contrast is an important element even in a neutral design scheme. Paint an accent wall at one end of the room, and add complementary pillows and lamps at the other end to create visual rhythm among spaces.

Chapter Seven

BLUEGRASS REVERIE

Working with friends and relatives can be tricky. Fortunately for me, my niece and her husband have asked me to help design and decorate several homes for them over the years with great results. So for their new home in western Kentucky, I was ecstatic when they asked me to help them create a home for their young family. My nephew-in-law, James, is a builder and had set apart some acreage for his family's dream home in the back parcel of a neighborhood he was developing near my hometown. I knew that he and my niece would appreciate the relaxed but charming Kentucky horse farm style, as it would embrace the faults and foibles of a busy young family. Needless to say, the couple loved this idea.

For new builds, I typically leave the siting of the home to the builder or architect. But for this project, James invited me to be hands-on throughout the process. James and I walked the property and looked from several vantage points for the best views, the most privacy and the most dramatic reveal from the property entrance.

The classic entrance features a circular staircase set against the backdrop of truffle-colored walls, with a round table situated in the center of the staircase nook. The chest in the foyer is from my niece's grandmother, and we found an antique Oushak runner to reflect the colors of the blue and white on the table.

For the design of the house, we tweaked a stock floor plan to accommodate the family's need for both work and play areas. There are a master and a guest suite on the main floor, with all the children's rooms on the second floor, along with a playroom and TV lounge. I enlarged the eat-in kitchen to accommodate both formal and informal dining and located the business office, in lieu of a formal dining room, immediately off the foyer. A mudroom was added between the main house and the garage, situating it on an angle in order to diminish the visual mass of the house, making it appear more cordial. With the mudroom entrance, the children can come in the house from the garage and go up to their rooms via a rear staircase that we added, making the house really work for this active family.

My niece and I have built four houses together over the years, so she trusts my taste and decisions, something I do not take for granted. During construction, I usually work more with her husband than with her, but for decorating the rooms in this, their dream home, she and I had much more interaction. I gave her a mood board with paint colors, fabrics, and wallcoverings to give her a sense of the overall look. Once she signed off on the general design direction, she let me go with the specifics.

The office for the family business is to the left of the foyer. To give it a more residential feel, I styled the office as a library, with a large bank of bookcases along the facing wall. My niece requested a bright peacock blue for the cabinetry, and I turned up the volume by painting all the trim in this room a vivid blue as well. This is a perfect counterpoint to the dark wall color that runs throughout most of the home. I selected a favorite Jacobean-style print for all the upholstery and window treatments. Placing the same fabric on everything in the room brought a sense of calm to the dynamic color scheme.

The great room is a vast two stories. I decided on a dark taupe color for most of the large public rooms so they felt more intimate and not imposing. The furnishings in the great room were selected with comfort and style in mind. A large sectional with a chaise on one end is situated in front of the stone fireplace, which also houses the TV. This arrangement is necessary for a room that works for young children and their insatiable appetite for cartoons, as well as for hosting sports viewing parties.

We added an upholstered ottoman as a cocktail table, covered in a tapestry reminiscent of an Oriental rug, and layered it on a bound broadloom area rug. (This is a trick I use a lot for young families on a budget to give the effect of—rather than spending a fortune on—a large Oriental-style rug.) The seating area is rounded out with a pair of club chairs in a geometric velvet and small armchairs we re-covered to fit the scheme, another gift from my niece's grandmother.

My niece has an affinity for white painted cabinets. So in the open kitchen and dining area, we added a porcelain backsplash that looks like Calacatta Gold marble but is more family friendly than real marble. I selected a large reproduction antique banquet table and paired it with a casual version of a Chippendale chair with rush seats. There is a small butler's pantry open to the dining area, which displays a collection of blue and white the couple has been gathering since they were married.

OPPOSITE: The dining area decor is casual enough for family meals yet can be dressed up for entertaining. Blue and white is a truly flexible color scheme.

Off the rear of the house is a covered porch, which we outfitted with deep seating in the same soft blue tones as the kitchen. This is a perfect perch from which to watch the kids play or to relax after a long day of work. A wonderful pale blue wicker sofa is just below the kitchen windows, which are often open to catch the breezes and so Mom can hear the children if they call.

The sofa is in a more modern silhouette for this young family, and cushions are in a gray-and-cream stripe. We placed a large table for outdoor dining and used a mix of chairs to give it a more relaxed look and feel. A long bench is at one end to accommodate more children when friends are over.

A mix of faux and real woven outdoor furniture sits on the covered porch. Mixing fabrics and finishes gives this outdoor space an eye-catching layered look.

The master bedroom is a complete departure in color scheme from the dark earth tones used in the rest of the house. Here the feeling is bright and fresh, a study in pale blue and cream, which sets it apart as a retreat, both physically and visually. For the window treatments and bedding, I chose a botanical, which is never out of style. The bedside chests—more heirlooms from my niece's grandmother—were given new life with a cream paint treatment to break up the "matchy" appearance and to correlate with the fabric in the room. Pale blue broadloom carpet was selected in a geometric pattern to infer a feeling of lattice, reinforcing the garden theme initiated by the botanical fabric.

This lattice theme is continued in the en suite bathroom, covering the walls in cream and aqua to complete the ethereal, courtyard feeling.

Working with my niece's family was a fulfilling experience. From design and construction to decorating and furnishing, our teamwork created a breathtaking abode that is an example of what can come from the camaraderie of close family. By choosing classic themes and livable fabrics, the interiors also will last the test of time.

OPPOSITE LEFT: A horse painting reinforces the Kentucky horse farm theme seen throughout the home.
OPPOSITE RIGHT: A collectible English case clock looks perfectly at home in this farmhouse, especially in view of the overstuffed chair wearing a casual blue-and-white pattern.
RIGHT: Nothing says well-worn like a brick floor. It adds instant age and never shows dirt.

Worth Noting

✳ Designing for busy families takes decorating from just picking pretty fabrics and finishes to selecting items that work easily with a family's lifestyle. In designing my niece's home, I specifically chose an exterior elevation design that spoke to a relaxed, rural aesthetic. The more casual facade means the house doesn't have to look perfectly dressed-up at all times. Strewn bicycles and toy wagons feel at home with a farm-style backdrop.

✳ The effectiveness of contrast cannot be overstated. If the walls are a dark color, add light-colored furniture and fabrics. The contrast creates visual interest and a dynamic effect in a room. This is true also of floors and rugs, as well as countertops and fabrics. There are exceptions, of course, but I almost always recommend contrasting colors when choosing finishes that easily live together.

Chapter Eight

RURAL ELEGANCE

I always say that creating something out of nothing is easy. Without the baggage of bad furniture or rugs with outdated color palettes, designers are able to create a perfect room and work magic outside the constraints of a client's previous bad buying decisions. It is when we have to work within the boundaries of a client's lifetime of collecting that we can get hamstrung. But these are the projects that I love the most! So, when a couple close to home contacted me to update the house on their family farm, I was excited to see what fresh take we could create with their existing furniture.

We met at their home, where I could see in situ the items that they either once loved or have loved for a lifetime. The stately country house was situated on the back portion of the family's once-large farm. You enter at the rear of the original farm and meander up a slow climb to the newer home, which is set among an expansive lawn and boxwood. The exterior was brick with a cove brick detail at the water table, just above the foundation. This small detail communicated to me that the client was keen on subtlety.

The generous foyer had a traditional green marble floor. There was a large pier-style mirror over a mahogany console, with an Oriental-style rug and a crystal chandelier hung in the center of the room. The sidelights and transom that surrounded the solid mahogany front door were beautifully proportioned to the space and I could tell were well thought out. However, the space was really bare-bones, and the finishes—or I should say, lack of finishes—left the space feeling empty. It just wasn't living up to its potential.

As the client walked me through the formal living room, it had a restrained feeling, lacked emotion; it wasn't telling a story. The Chippendale sofa, wing chair and English Gothic secretary were all stately and tasteful, but the carpet was beige and unmemorable. The room was in the center of an enfilade of rooms, the last being the dining room, which had the traditional but austere mahogany suite of table, chairs, buffet and server. To the rear of the dining room was the entrance to the breakfast room, which had all-white-painted vintage furniture and an abundance of daylight flooding through the bank of sizable windows. I knew immediately that this room needed a dark color to absorb the light and reduce the glare.

Our tour went on through the kitchen and ended in the family room. My task, stated at the end of the meeting, was to update the rooms with new colors and fabrics but to use the majority of the furnishings the client already owned. "Just make everything fresh," she said.

Here is where I really love to work! My sweet spot in design is to take an inventory of a client's past purchases and create an entirely new feeling out of the old items. I quickly set about the task of laying out the rooms in new arrangements.

In the large dining room, I selected a popular bird pattern in sepia tones for the walls. Again, I used the client's trellis-patterned tone-on-tone area rug, as well as all of their existing dark wood furniture. The cream of the rug against the brown furniture repeated the brown-and-cream color scheme of the wallpaper. As a counterpoint, I added coral and cream, embroidered damask host chairs at either end of the table and introduced candy-colored watercolor art on the walls. This gave the room a jovial nature while retaining its formality.

OPPOSITE: A pair of vintage tole painted lamps sit atop an antique server. **ABOVE:** Perfectly polished silver from the homeowner's collection sparkles in the new dining room.

The breakfast room is just behind the dining room, so I wanted there to be a visual relationship between the two rooms. I painted the walls of the breakfast room the same custom chocolate that I used for the walls below the chair rail in the dining room.

It was also an ideal foil for blue-and-white Chinese export porcelain. A blue-and-white-print curtain fabric with a terra-cotta paisley was the superb fabric to link the blue-and-white with the corals and terra-cottas in the other rooms. The final fabric was a charming brown-and-white gingham, to layer a bit of country into this pretty room.

ABOVE: The furniture in the breakfast room was a vintage set the homeowner had previously painted white. The client did not own any blue-and-white porcelain (gasp!), so we found her an instant collection that looked utterly elegant on her vintage baker's rack. **OPPOSITE:** Dark truffle walls are the perfect foil for blue-and-white accents.

Choosing the colors for the family room, which is in the center of the suite of rooms and bordered by a covered porch, was a bit of a challenge due to the lack of natural light. I wanted a neutral wall but was afraid the lack of light would make it feel cold. I decided on a sisal wallcovering, whose rough texture brought more depth and visual interest, especially as a background for all the fine antique pieces.

The lead print fabric for the window treatments and a reproduction French-style chair is a cotton chintz with birds on a fig-colored ground. I love purple, but the deep aubergine leaves lean more toward brown, which references the brown tones that I have used in other rooms. The figgy brown ground also adds depth to the overall look of the house, keeping the colors from being too matchy, or flat. I also found a wonderful cognac-colored velvet to pair with the cotton chintz and give a nice texture. I'm not a fan of leather, so I like to use velvet as an alternative to introduce a similar texture to leather. The combinations in this room help give the overall scheme a masculine note.

FACING ABOVE: I found a texture that resembles some contrived animal print I've never seen in nature, to cover a pair of bobbin chairs in a light finish that contrasts nicely with the client's existing tobacco-colored Welsh cupboard. FACING LEFT: We found a stunning case clock for the family room to bring a sense of age and permanence. Antique tall case clocks are like living things in the home—temperamental, quirky and finicky. They only work when they want to. But the ticktock is soothing, like the rhythm of a heartbeat.

The icing on the cake with this project was that it was redesigned to be ready in time for the clients' daughter's pending nuptials. While it wasn't the setting for the wedding, the family would be welcoming many out-of-town relatives and friends, using the home as a backdrop to the festivities. The owners were thrilled that visitors commented on how the home looked updated while also reflecting the personal style and taste of the client. It was rewarding to see how thankful the couple was that we had used so many of their family pieces. The fresh, updated rooms made the clients and their newly extended family excited to start the next chapter in their lives together.

Worth Noting

* Keep in mind that the foyer sets the tone of your house. Think of it as a prelude or overture, giving hints of what's to come. Try to repeat colors from other rooms in a rug, fabric or wallcovering as linking elements to create unity and balance in the home's decor.

* While we often hear that lighter paint colors make a room feel larger, sometimes dark colors can work, for other reasons. If you get a lot of sunlight in a room, a dark wall will help absorb the light and reduce glare. This is particularly effective in rooms where items seem backlit by the sun. By reducing glare, items in the room are more noticeable and the room is easier on the eyes.

Chapter Nine

BLUE BLOOD AERIE

High on a hill above the mélange of old and new suburban residences south of Nashville sits a spectacular home filled with a mix of traditional fabrics and furnishings designed to convey a noble spirit for a small family of three. Soaring ceilings and spacious rooms are resplendent with heavy architectural moldings and details fit for a house on Embassy Row. And the only thing that competes with the large, lushly filled rooms is a tremendous view of the rolling hills of middle Tennessee. But this magnificent home had a rough start to have ended in such regalia. This is truly a rags to riches story.

The custom-built house was approximately twenty years old when my clients purchased it. Unfortunately, trim details were nonexistent in several rooms and the quality of the finishings was deficient. The rooms were quite large and felt extremely out of proportion to human scale. I set about designing rooms that would create a sense of grandeur and intimacy so that the small family wouldn't be swallowed up by the immense house.

My modus operandi is to do the decorating first; then I can see where to spend money on the architecture. Of course, if you have an endless budget, then indeed change everything. But in my experience, everyone has a budget. Think, *Where can I get the biggest bang for my buck? Do I need to spend a fortune tearing off bad moldings and redesigning door and window surrounds, or would a properly scaled window treatment bring better proportions between the window and the room?* When you look at rooms this way, you can spend your money more efficiently. I do this so my clients actually have money left to spend on gorgeous window treatments and antique rugs!

Another interesting part of this story is that the wife didn't want to use any of their current furnishings because neither she nor her husband liked how any of the rooms in their previous home looked or functioned, so there was some baggage attached to those furnishings. She thought they were too big, too casual, uncomfortable, and not pretty enough for the Southern-and-traditional-style home that she envisioned. But I knew that in the right context, her current collection could be beautiful and functional in her new home.

My work began in the foyer. It had a wainscoting that encompassed the room, so at least there was already some visual heft in this two-story entry. The flooring was a cold Carrara marble, which didn't help the grand room feel approachable. It opened onto the grand salon, which had absolutely no molding, save the mantel and a basic baseboard. I planned to really turn up the architectural details in the salon, so I decided to restrain from adding more molding in the foyer but rather replace the marble floor with new hardwood to create more warmth.

An antique Oushak runner in blue and terra-cotta, along with a sideboard from the clients' collection, dressed up the foyer.

Looking right, the music room was simply surrounded in drywall. The client wanted everything light and bright, but the home still needed a dark color of contrast amid the bright foyer and what would be a very formal grand salon. The music room was to feel more masculine. For this effect, I selected a pecky cypress to clad the walls and had a dark espresso furniture finish applied. This was much more than just staining the walls: it gave them a translucent quality that you only get with a multistep finish accomplished by a talented painter.

For decorating this room, aside from the piano, the clients had a pair of wing chairs and a French-style reproduction chest that I incorporated with a new rug and window treatments.

OPPOSITE: An antique Oushak rug leads the eye through the foyer and to the tremendous view. **ABOVE LEFT:** The music room walls are a moody counterpoint to the light colors used elsewhere in the home. **ABOVE RIGHT:** An antique Italian footstool is paired with the client's existing wing chair. The mix elevates everything in the music room.

The grand salon features the majestic view of lush, green, rolling hills at the rear of the home, a certain showstopper. We reused the clients' Oriental-style area rug, which matched the new fabrics perfectly, as well as her club chairs, tables and a large buffet.

To make the room feel really grand, I selected an overscaled Empire-style beaded chandelier (see page 138) and added more trim to the overmantel, as well as wainscoting on the clerestory to fill in the weird angles of the vaulted ceiling. By creating a clean, straight line at ten feet, the visual noise of the slopes and valleys of the ceiling have been diminished, allowing a quieter interior to enjoy the rolling vista.

OPPOSITE: With the verdant view outside the window in mind, I selected a large-scale hydrangea print in pale celadon for the lead fabric of this room, using it for window treatments and pulling all its light, airy color tones onto the walls and furnishings.

In the kitchen, which is separated from the grand salon but open to the large den, we changed the dingy cream cabinetry to a cleaner white and painted the walls a crisp neutral in a shade of flaxen. New furnishings here had a decidedly European aesthetic. The bistro chairs had a French flair, while the large, tavern-style table had a chippy paint finish in a Swedish style.

The kitchen windows were the most out of proportion in the home. The transom loomed large over a series of five casement-style windows. While this allowed for more of the amazing view, the size was so domineering that you couldn't focus on the view. I designed a large but simple window treatment in a sweetly scaled floral toss pattern of lemons, herbs and greenery to break the large expanse of banked windows into smaller sections, creating better proportions for the room. The tableau of the large table, chairs and print fabric is visually impressive but restful at the same time.

OPPOSITE: The house has excellent flow and sight lines from room to room but also allows privacy when necessary. RIGHT: Mixing finishes from casual to formal helps give the breakfast area a dynamic look.

A large den, off the kitchen, needed to be functional for the small family of three but also accommodate large parties. An Arts and Crafts influence seemed appropriate since there was an existing stacked-stone fireplace. We painted the walls in a moody dark green, which also brought the walls in and gave an intimacy to this family space. The clients' existing Oriental-style rug, a pair of sofas and a menagerie of antique tables were brought in to the furniture arrangement.

My favorite French-style bergère chair in green velvet makes for a quiet sitting corner where guests can really take in the tremendous view. The complete effect is a room for both intimate comfort and cocktail parties with more guests.

Window treatments in a William Morris–inspired print of a whirling leaf pattern coupled with drapery panels in a mini vine print, which all hung on mahogany drapery hardware, gave a masculine touch and added a sense of traditional formality.

The master bedroom was one of the most uncomfortable rooms I have ever entered. It was so long and narrow that it felt like a bowling alley—not physically narrow but visually narrow when compared to its exaggerated length. The remedy was adding an entablature across the room to demarcate the bedroom from the sitting area, which gave the bed chamber a better proportion and also created beautiful interest in the room. This grand architectural gesture also gave context to the tall, double-tray ceiling and existing iron-and-crystal chandelier.

I designed a sweeping canopy for the bed in a combination of aquamarine and chocolate toile paired with a coordinated plaid and tassel trim for a fully Southern traditional effect. We layered in the client's existing bed and a sofa and chairs that looked completely at home in their new environment.

OPPOSITE: A hoop skirt is the only thing more Southern than a canopy bed. This canopy combines floral and plaid to imbue an elegant effect. **RIGHT:** Collections of creamware and antique French journal pages add a sense of history to the master bedroom.

The second floor of the house had several public areas, a large loft at the top of the rear stairs and two large office areas. The loft is really a large hallway transitioning between the bedrooms and the offices. The area acts as an axis point as you travel around the various spaces of the second floor, so I wanted it to be not just a hallway but a visual experience. This was a great space to display a collection of blue-and-white Chinese export porcelain. The clients' own marquetry chest was used as a dark counterpoint to the light-filled space and was topped with their white French-style mirror.

The clients wanted an office for him and an office for her. I asked the wife, with whom I have a jovial relationship, "Do you need a space to work from home?" and she said, "No, I just need a place to visit with friends and drink champagne." So, naturally, we named her office the Champagne Room. I kept the colors feminine and pretty, because that, of course, is the perfect backdrop for drinking champagne!

I found a treillage-style broadloom carpet and a spearmint-and-white ticking stripe to cover most of the furniture and windows. For a couture touch, a floral embroidered band decorates the slipper chairs and window treatments.

LEFT: A large hall is the perfect place to show off a selection of the client's Chinese export porcelain, old and new. OPPOSITE: The "Champagne Room" is set up to have cocktails. The shelves are styled with the client's personal collection of objects.

Dearly Loved
CHANEL

AMERICAN DIOR

SIMPLICITY IS
THE KEYNOTE
OF ALL TRUE
ELEGANCE
-COCO CHANEL

The husband's office, on the other hand, oozes masculinity. Against a backdrop of dark juniper green walls and trim, I mixed colored fabrics, textures and patterns, many times on a single piece of upholstery.

The outcome of this renovation and redecoration project was beyond the high expectations of my clients. By not only renovating a diamond in the rough but also utilizing their own collection of furnishings to look better in their new surroundings, the family is able to enjoy the stunning panorama outside as well as the beautiful views throughout the rooms of their treetop home.

This gentleman's lounge allows him to work comfortably from home and to entertain guests and colleagues in luxury when necessary. Who would ever want to leave such enjoyment?

Worth Noting

* Need inspiration for creating color schemes in your home? Let nature help you create your color palette. Look outside at the views from your rooms to find colors that will mix well with your interiors. Rooms are made richer when they complement the exterior views they take in.

* Consider which pieces of furniture in your current collection would look completely different in a new environment. Changing the backdrop that your furniture is part of is a big change, and elevating humble pieces with luxurious new fabrics can take your sofa, for instance, from sad to sublime in no time.

* When starting a renovation project, you don't always need to begin with a clean slate. Sometimes adding to can be more effective than taking away. This is especially true of architectural trim details. Instead of ripping out a small baseboard, consider adding a small bead of trim above it to make it appear larger. Once you paint the old and new trim the same color, the visual effect will be one larger, more ornamented molding.

Chapter Ten

ENGLISH COUNTRY CHARM

More than fifteen years ago, a prospective client came to the design studio I was running at the time for another designer and asked me to help her with a whole-house renovation. We met the next week and began renovations of her kitchen and bathrooms as well as developing design schemes for the living areas and bedrooms so they would coordinate with the new finishes we were selecting. We completed the project in less than six weeks and the client was thrilled with the outcome. But that's not the end of the story. We have redecorated that house three times in the years since! You know what they say: the third time's the charm.

The wife and I have complementary taste, and we work together during the installation of the new rooms. She has a fantastic eye and is such a help that I lean on her as a design assistant when installing her rooms. I'll say, "This table could use a small stack of boxes," and she'll run to her storage stash of treasures and return with ten to choose from! Her attic is better than any gift shop I've ever been to.

All three versions of the home were enchanting and endearing in their various iterations. The first one featured rich, bright colors. The second version focused on reupholstering fabrics and rugs to fit within the wall finishes. This current version was a complete reimagining of the rooms, using quieter, neutral color palettes with subtle notes of color so the house has a fresher feel.

The client has an amazing collection of upholstery and wood furniture that we have either recovered, restored or painted to make pieces look older or more expensive. It's always fun to take a piece someone has had for many years and reimagine it with a different finish or patina and place it somewhere new in the house so it looks completely fresh in a new environment.

The house has eight-foot ceilings, which can cast some dreary shadows. To counteract this, I chose a shimmery wallcovering in the foyer in a silver grasscloth to brighten up the small space. This neutral color also made it easy to create various color schemes for the attached rooms. I also replaced the client's Wilton-style floral stair runner with a black-and-cream leopard print. My adoration for animal prints is well documented, and with the black hand rail that we painted fifteen years ago, the little bit of black in the leopard carpet added a contemporary, of-the-moment feel.

The first room seen from the foyer is the living room. It has always had a small camelback sofa, but the arrangement of furniture has changed several times. This time, the sofa lives in front of a chinoiserie-inspired floor screen that doubles as art. We upholstered all the furniture in a menagerie of neutrals, with nailhead details to add texture and interest. The window treatments and pillows sport a large-scale floral print fabric in watercolor pastels.

Open to the living room, the formal dining room is now cladded in wood paneling that is painted a linen white, which is almost the color of an undercooked biscuit. The color changes from pale gray to a dried parchment as the sunlight changes.

The client's wonderful collection of blue-and-white Chinese export porcelain prompted the color scheme for this room. To tie in the blue, we selected a French knot–style embroidered curtain in cream with touches of blue and covered the dining chair seats in a newer version of a gold-and-cream flame stitch to complement.

For the host chairs, we splurged on a linen-and-silk lampas fabric depicting two Asian sailors and punctuated the elegant lines of the chairs with a mini flange in plaid. The room is scattered with other blue and white, which is a lovely counterpoint to the large equine portrait over the buffet.

One room we did not need to update on this third rendition of the family home is the sunroom, which we added almost five years ago and which the family uses most. The room continues the cream color palette but injects apple green to bring the outdoors inside.

The views from this room are outstanding, and I created several different zones where they can be enjoyed. On one end of the room is a desk to be utilized as a workstation with space for a laptop; it can double as a small bar for prepping drinks. The center of the room is the lounging area, with a large cast-limestone fireplace on one side and a wall of cabinetry on the other, housing the TV. On the far end, a small bistro table is a lovely spot for morning coffee or a light lunch. When there are just two to dine, it makes a nice alternative to the large, formal dining room or casual kitchen. I do love to squeeze in extra places to eat if I can in a floor plan, because these become special places a client wouldn't utilize otherwise. And the vista to the yard is particularly splendid from this table.

OPPOSITE: Blue and white accents in lamps and other objets d'art are linking elements to the other rooms of the house.

The kitchen we designed seventeen years ago was still functioning well for the family—a testament to classic style. All we did this time was to clean up the accessories by removing some random vignette displays of tole-ware and using only cream as our color palette for collectibles. We kept the wallcovering, window treatments, chandelier and furniture. We retained the custom-painted cabinets from the original design for a personalized touch. By simplifying the arrangement of accessories and pulling into service the client's collection of creamware from various storage places in the home, we made the kitchen look current.

This home has a delightful outdoor space just beyond the kitchen. Its proximity makes the outdoor dining area one of the most used areas for family gatherings. For this space, we changed the outdoor curtains from a solid celadon to a brown-and-beige awning stripe, which we fabricated on the horizontal to give it an edgier vibe. A natural teak dining table was paired with outdoor rush-and-iron chairs. Mixing materials keeps the outdoor dining space from feeling too new.

OPPOSITE: Mixing materials is a trick I employ a lot in outdoor areas, because using all the same woven wicker or iron or teak feels like the room was purchased new and not collected over time. On the other hand, a layered effect of different materials creates a laid-back look, which is especially desirable for an outdoor room.

Another great space we refined was the TV lounge. This room holds the largest TV in the house, for sports watching and time with extended family.

The family has a love affair with dogs. We installed a wallcovering many years ago with a dog motif, which we decided to keep with our refresh, but opted to change the dark-stained poplar trim to a painted gray. This, along with installing new carpet in a light oatmeal wool, modernized the feel of the room. This room is a testament to the power of curating the right accessories and was a joy to decorate with my client's many dog collectibles. I even filled a glass container with dog biscuits for the grand-dogs.

The master bedroom was the last room to update, and we really splurged on beautiful carpet and fabrics. The room is compact in size and has a small fireplace to the side. The furniture placement in this space has always been difficult, but this time it was even more challenging because the client wanted a king-size bed. I found delicate bedside chests that let us gain space for a larger bed. We also went with a wicker chair because seeing through it makes it seem smaller than it is. The mix of embroidered textiles and fabrics printed in India completed the quiet color scheme.

Without a doubt, the reimagining of this family home was a treat to design and decorate. By looking for lighter fabrics and finishes and incorporating timeless heirlooms from the client's personal collection, the home feels like it's been this way for many years.

LEFT: A vignette of antique bird prints provides a link to nature that the homeowners love.
OPPOSITE: The mix of paisley with other fabrics gives a sense of ease in the master bedroom.

Worth Noting

* Redecorating your home doesn't require a Herculean effort. Take the upholstery and furniture you currently have and do a toss-up of all the pieces. Imagine you have moved into a new home and how you can move pieces into different rooms with new fabrics, rugs and wallcoverings. You can create something truly new out of the old.

* Curating a collection of objects takes many years, if not a lifetime. In my experience, clients never have enough items to make their homes feel layered. Layering is what gives the home a sense of history—the homeowner's history. Look around your home for objects that resonate with you and buy more that will complement them. A perfectly placed collection is the mark of a genuinely sophisticated home.

Chapter Eleven

THE SUBURBAN CHIC HOME

A colleague of a longtime client reached out for my help in creating a new home for her family from a house that was outdated and lacked any real character. Their only child was going away to college, and they wanted to upgrade their home to be more conducive to adult living. The client wanted to do a quick update without heroic renovations. She wanted to move into the house in one month, so there was no time for major renovations. Her only directives were to repaint, replace two small kitchen islands for one large island, and renovate the master bathroom so it looked more up-to-date.

The house, in a lovely suburban neighborhood with other large homes built during the housing boom of the early 2000s, was lacking in "special touches." Overall, it had great bones, but the client was correct in wanting to change the kitchen island and the master bathroom; both were in need of a total redo. The rest just needed to be refreshed and refined with new paint and some architectural millwork.

My priority was to make the house more detailed and bring in fixtures that were scaled appropriately for the space. In my estimation, the problems in this house started in the two-story foyer. It had a beautiful curving staircase with delicately scrolled ironwork. But the chandelier was seriously huge; it dominated the space and belonged in a large hotel. Also, there was too much drywall. Since the domed ceiling was twenty-four feet in the air, the drywall extended uninterrupted almost as high. This grand foyer opened onto the great room without cased openings separating the spaces. All of this vast space created a "sea of drywall."

My goal in any home is to create an intimate and comfortable space. To that end, I set about adding millwork throughout the clerestory of this immense space to break up the drywall monotony. Adding the paneled trim details brought the space down to a more human scale. I also replaced the colossal chandelier with a much smaller iron-and-crystal chandelier from the existing dining room and hung it much lower in the space as well. Now it is in the line of sight when you enter.

In the kitchen, I created a new layout for one large island where previously there had been two smaller ones that segmented the kitchen work space and alienated guests. In this day and age, the kitchen is paramount in any home design. People use it as a setting for entertaining, so a kitchen needs to accommodate guests as well as function for meal preparation and efficient cleanup. We reoriented the new larger island 90 degrees, which allowed space for more barstools and gave the kitchen a cleaner, updated look. I coated all the dark cabinetry in the perfect shade of white paint and installed new quartz countertops and marble backsplash to finish the reboot to the heart of the home.

ABOVE: We salvaged the existing cartouche above the range from the previous backsplash. It adds a traditional element to the updated kitchen.

OPPOSITE: A small breakfast area is dressed with French bistro chairs surrounding a round table with whimsically shaped supports.

Color choices played a particularly important role because this house's position toward the sun made the light dull in some very important rooms. The kitchen, family room and master bedroom were all dark and somber, while the center of the house—the foyer, center gallery and great room—had wonderful sunlight. The foyer and gallery also had a beautiful beige marble floor that I used as inspiration for the wall color in these spaces, creating a neutral central nave for the house.

When I encounter light quality as dim as the light in the left and right wings of this house, I always go to a clean, clear color palette. Blue can pierce a drab light problem faster than any other color. I balanced the left and right of the center foyer in shades of blue: more celadon in the master suite and hydrangea blue in the dining room. Blue would play a role as a counterpoint to the cooler earth tone I selected as the overall color. This effectively bounced what little light there was around the rooms as much as possible.

The dining room is quite large, so I knew it would be a challenge to make the space feel intimate. I chose a wallcovering that is a tone-on-tone wisteria vine in a shade I call hydrangea—like the blue in a true French hydrangea—and for contrast I added touches of green in the kitchen, moving to more olive tones with blue accents in the family room.

The dining room is alive with pattern. We kept the carved crown molding and added French touches by way of the lantern and mirror. The bunny weather vane is from the homeowner's collection.

OPPOSITE: A mix of menswear fabrics was used in the den to create a handsome place to relax. ABOVE LEFT: A peacock blue chenille is paired with a floral print on the den sofas. ABOVE RIGHT: A wool paisley covers the cocktail ottoman.

OPPOSITE: An ethereal painting is the scene setter in the master bedroom. **ABOVE:** We added a lighter mood to the previously dark and moody master bedroom by changing the paint, carpet and furnishings.

In the master bath, the cabinetry was in great shape. But the tub area was completely oversized, with a large bulkhead supported by enormous Roman columns, which we simply removed. This was a much cheaper and faster option than gutting the bathroom and starting over. We resurfaced the tub deck, floors and shower in a white marble and porcelain painted accent tile used en masse, which yielded a luxurious and decadent feel to the bathroom and made it seem larger.

All that was left to do was paint the walls pale blue-gray, giving it a crispness it didn't have before—although getting that perfect shade of blue took five tries! The light is terribly drab in that bathroom and colors looked different there than they did in the bedroom; getting both rooms to look the same was a test. Mercifully, my client was patient as we searched and tried different shades until we landed on the perfect tint.

OPPOSITE: For a peaceful feeling, I designed all the fabrics to be calm and quiet in the master. **ABOVE:** A glazed chintz window treatment makes the windows around the tub look taller and creates better proportions in the master bath.

The combination of adding appropriate lighting and millwork, simplifying the kitchen layout, renovating the master bathroom, and updating the paint colors made a chic new home for these empty-nesters. They now enjoy entertaining family and friends in their sophisticated, mature rooms. These updates have given new life and a spirit of elegance to a suburban house that was waiting to be correctly jeweled in the finery of a European house.

OPPOSITE: The great room is a study in neutrals. The change in textures from rug to coffee table, upholstery, walls and accessories adds drama to the space.

Worth Noting

If you have a suburban home that's lacking in character, here's what you can do:

✳ In rooms taller than ten feet, break it up with millwork. Look for rooms where you can add or highlight architecture with trim.

✳ If your room is lacking major architectural elements, like a fireplace or cabinetry, add six-inch beadboard to the walls, or apply panel moldings. This will give a bland room more style and panache than any color of paint alone.

Chapter Twelve

URBAN GENTRY

I always wanted to live in an old home. The materials used to build homes a hundred years ago were better quality, so old homes have a sense of permanence that new homes lack. Their history also shrouds them in a cloud of mystery. With every step through an old home, every creak of the floor and mirage seen through wavy glass, I can create a backstory about previous lives lived under one historic roof.

My family and I became part of history when we found our new old Georgian-style home, Boxwood Hill. The park-like setting with more than a hundred trees was situated on $2\frac{1}{2}$ acres in the middle of a city going through a renaissance. Two Cape Cod cottage–style guesthouses on the rear of the property meant we were buying an entire estate.

Boxwood Hill had had a major renovation in 2008, during which the electrical, plumbing and HVAC systems, insulation and roof were updated and footage was added to the kitchen. Fortunately for us, we were able to spend our resources on the decorative elements that would make the house sing.

When my wife, Ruthann, and I first looked at the house, she decided it wasn't for her. The rooms were laid out in a traditional floor plan, with the

kitchen addition extending off the back and separated from the living spaces by a staircase wall. Ruthann felt she would spend too much time apart from the family if she were in the kitchen preparing meals and we were in a separate room.

While at a meeting for another renovation, the client had asked me to add a rear staircase in her new home, and the builder had responded that it would be no problem at all. This gave me the inspiration that we could make Boxwood Hill work for our family by removing the rear staircase to create one large kitchen/breakfast room/family room space. There was also space for a bathroom and closet addition atop the flat roof outside a large bedroom, which would create en-suite bathrooms for all the bedrooms.

Seeing that all of our wants could be met in this house, I began refining the interior details. Boxwood Hill is not a grand house. It has a noble facade, but the rooms are intimate and delicately scaled. The previous renovation incorporated details seen in grand European homes, not charming American homes, of which this is one. I seek authenticity in my designs and wanted the rooms to appear as if they had always existed in their current state. I used restraint when redesigning mantels, making them smaller but classically detailed. I added molding to the dining room and simplified the trim details from the kitchen cabinetry. The remaining staircase in the front entrance had a pair of volutes that were far too large for the small foyer. I replaced them with a simpler, vase-style newel post and exchanged the heavy iron stair pickets with simple Doric-style wood ones, indicative of the original period and style of the home. To give more detail and heft to the family room, I added pecky cypress beams and facade to an existing built-in. I also cladded pecky cypress to an existing vaulted ceiling in the breakfast room, creating a visual link between these now attached rooms.

An English townhouse theme was appropriate for Boxwood Hill due to its small size. City townhouses are small but their interiors are impeccably dressed, so the focus is on details and refinement, starting with the doors. I wanted all the interior doors to be painted British racing green because it pairs well with the redbrick exterior.

Next came the furnishings. For the living room, I decided to use a colorful, much-loved Sultanabad rug from our previous home. To prevent the colors overtaking the room, I chose neutral fabrics for the window treatments and upholstery, and a tooled leather chinoiserie screen as a focal point over the green velvet sofa. The combination is a buttoned-up attitude, but also refreshing with the addition of cotton bullion fringe at the skirt of the sofa, a classic and current trend.

LEFT: A couple of antique bergère chairs are paired with a Lucite-top table. The small chair in the background belonged to Ruthann's mother. **ABOVE:** A modern-style end table and lamp keep the living room from feeling stuffy.

At the end of the living room, French doors open into Ruthann's office. She wanted a blue room, so I painted all the existing dark cherry wood cabinetry and trim in robin's-egg blue and chose pale aquamarine grasscloth for the walls, complemented by a flora and fauna print fabric for the window treatments. Together we found an antique writing desk for her work space and an oversized French bergère chair, which has become more dog bed than chair, since both of our dogs like to nap on it. Ruthann selected a cream-and-brown leopard print carpet that I had surged in robin's-egg blue thread to complement the new cabinet color. The effect is like the interior of a jewel box.

PREVIOUS OVERLEAF: The living room showcases a collection of old and new furnishings. **OPPOSITE:** We found the settee while antiquing together. The plates are a set from Ruthann's grandmother. **ABOVE:** An antique desk placed near a window is dreamy spot from which to view the property.

In the family room, I painted the walls and trim a dark, velvety green and paired it with a combination of wool plaid and floral chintz in various shades of blue, green and deep chocolate. Our collection of blue-and-white Chinese export porcelain shines in this space. Blue and white has been our color scheme since we married.

OPPOSITE: The valance fabric was the inspiration for the color palette of the entire house and is one of my favorites. **ABOVE:** The stately English case clock is just around the corner from the shelves that hold books and other treasures.

The dining room has been painted in a white semigloss to highlight the new panel molding and make the petite room appear larger than it is. I installed a favorite Italian crystal chandelier that has hung in three of our houses over the last fifteen years, incorporating not only a family treasure but a tried-and-true trick of decorating: add sparkle to a room that is small because bouncing light fools the eye and makes the room appear larger.

Our breakfast room and kitchen are open to the den and I wanted to create a country kitchen there. I found the perfect-size check fabric in beige and biscuit to cover the walls, windows and chairs. The resulting effect is both dramatic and amiable—not a simple task. An antique brass lantern from England, now electrified, holds court over our kitchen table, which is surrounded with a set of reproduction New England–style wicker chairs. I used our collection of blue and white throughout the kitchen and breakfast room. Some of our favorite pieces sit atop a linen press that Ruthann and I purchased at our first auction together.

OPPOSITE: The linen press first served as our daughter's changing table in her nursery and stands imposingly against the fabric wallcovering.

Our daughter, Julianne, and I worked together to decorate her bedroom, which was a unique experience. It needed to reflect her teen style and also be something I would enjoy looking at. She developed a mood board of looks she liked, and she really wanted navy and coral. I love coral as well and was happily surprised at her choice.

To accent a navy bedspread, I found a small-scale print in coral, cream and navy for the curtains and dust ruffle. A navy and white rug made the room feel youthful, and a bold stripe created a strong accent wall behind the bed, giving the room energy and panache. Julianne and I were both very pleased with the result.

LEFT: This is the brightest room in the house and we love it! The love seat we slipcovered is from Julianne's great-grandparents. We reused the desk and bedside tables from her previous room and painted the drawer fronts to coordinate.

A pair of consoles skirted in green tea garden chinoiserie greets people as they head upstairs to the bedrooms. Window treatments are in the same fabric. Since blue and green is my favorite color combination, I chose a blue and cream striped grasscloth wallcovering. The fresh color scheme turned what would have been a boring hallway into a room unto itself.

In the master suite at the end of the hall, I took a total departure from my normal aesthetic and went neutral. The fabric for the bed canopy—a print with lettuce green flowers on a cream ground—inspired the color scheme. The canopy is lined in a green and cream pinstripe that is repeated on the dust skirt and lampshades. Since the bedroom is small by today's standards, I covered the walls in a subtle tone-on-tone mini stripe that almost looks hand drawn. A beautiful Oushak rug completed the soft look and romantic feel.

RIGHT: The color scheme here is restful and reminiscent of the outdoors. Fabrics soften the entire room, including the head- and footboards.

Worth Noting

✳ Never underestimate the power of a painted door. I use them in many of my projects, since colorful paint highlights the architecture of the door more than white paint would and creates a layered effect. Painting bland doors adds drama and is a great way to update them without having to replace them altogether, an expensive proposition.

✳ Even without increasing square footage, you can improve flow in a home. Consider if a room just needs an easy change, such as removing a wall or widening an opening to increase the line of sight. By allowing you to see from one room to the next, rooms feel even larger.

Boxwood Hill is now a perfect embodiment of "tradition meets modern living." By opening up the floor plan, adding modern conveniences and refining the home's historic details, Boxwood Hill has become a home that our family will enjoy for many years, a legacy for generations to come. This stately home and grounds represent the classic tradition of Southern style so esteemed in the Nashville community.

Complementing the soft palette of the bedroom, the master bathroom was covered in a cream-and-gold metallic peony wallcovering. An antique Italian fountain remnant placed in front of a window blocks the unsightly view of the black asphalt roof. The combined effect is like being in a garden.

RECOMMENDED

Some of my favorite shops and sources:

CANTERBURY COTTAGE ANTIQUES
Nashville, TN

J & D ORIENTAL RUGS
New York, NY

HEDGEROW ANTIQUES
Atlanta, GA

NORTHGATE GALLERY INC.
Brentwood, TN; Chattanooga, TN

CK SWAN
Highlands, NC

CAROLINE FAISON ANTIQUES
Greensboro, NC

WINCHESTER ANTIQUE MALL
Franklin, TN

VIVIANNE METZGER ANTIQUES
Cashiers, NC

DALTON BAIN
DaltonBain.com

WATSON FLOOR GALLERY
Brentwood, TN

SUMMER PLACE ANTIQUES
Cashiers, NC

PICKWICK ANTIQUES
Montgomery, AL

PERSIAN GALLERIES
Brentwood, TN

DELRAY & ASSOCIATES
Atlanta, GA

First Edition
21 20 19 18 17   5 4 3 2 1
Text © 2018 Eric Ross
Photographs © 2018 Evin Krehbiel
End sheet courtesy Thibault

Published by
Gibbs Smith
P.O. Box 667
Layton, Utah 84041
1.800.835.4993 orders
www.gibbs-smith.com

Designed by Rita Sowins / Sowins Design
Page production by Virginia Brimhall Snow
Printed and bound in Hong Kong

Gibbs Smith books are printed on either recycled, 100% post-consumer waste, FSC-certified papers or on paper produced from sustainable PEFC-certified forest/controlled wood source. Learn more at www.pefc.org.

Library of Congress Cataloging-in-Publication Data

Names: Ross, Eric, 1972- author.
Title: Enduring Southern homes / Eric Ross ; photographs by Evin Krehbiel.
Description: First edition. | Layton, Utah : Gibbs Smith, [2019]
Identifiers: LCCN 2018033192 | ISBN 9781423650690 (jacketed hardcover)
Subjects: LCSH: Interior decoration--Southern States.
Classification: LCC NK2006 .R67 2019 | DDC 747.0975--dc23
LC record available at https://lccn.loc.gov/2018033192